VOLUNTEER
YOUTH
WORKERS
Recruiting and Developing
Leaders for Youth Ministry

◆

by J. David Stone and
Rose Mary Miller

Volunteer Youth Workers

Copyright © 1985 by J. David Stone and Rose Mary Miller

Second Printing

Library of Congress Cataloging in Publication Data

Stone, J. David.
  Volunteer youth workers.

  1. Church work with youth.   2. Christian leadership.
  I. Miller, Rose Mary, 1949-
BV4447.S716   1984   259'.2   84-82401
ISBN 0931-529-02-6 (pbk.)

CREDITS
Edited by Cindy S. Hansen
Designed by Jean Bruns
Front cover photos by David Strickler
Back cover photo by Jim Whitmer

CONTENTS

◆

ABOUT THE AUTHORS

◆

J. David Stone is the executive director of Youth Ministries Consultation Service, Shreveport, Louisiana, which provides resources and leadership training to many churches across the nation. He has served more than 25 years as a youth ministries professional.

David has authored several youth ministries handbooks, **Friend to Friend** (Group Books), and several video cassettes. He is a frequent contributor to many youth ministry publications, including GROUP Magazine.

David lives in Shreveport with his wife, Sissy, and three daughters: Mitzi, Karen and Carlana.

Rose Mary Miller is the associate director of Youth Ministries Consultation Service. She began working in youth ministry 14 years ago as a volunteer youth worker.

Rose Mary is married to Don, a high school coach and her biggest fan and supporter, and has three children: Toby, Natalie and Matt.

We dedicate this book to our children.

◆

- Mitzi, Karen and Carlana Stone
- Toby, Natalie and Matt Miller

PREFACE

◆

Some people believe, "When youth ministry becomes a priority in the church, there is heavy adult involvement." Others insist, "When there is heavy adult involvement, youth ministry becomes a priority in the church."

That's a paradox! Which comes first? Youth ministry or adult involvement? Many churches place adult involvement first. They believe that they first need total adult support of the youth program complete with counselors, director and officers.

We believe that a strong priority in youth ministry and a visible, active group come first. Then, the adults will see the excitement of this ministry, be interested in it, and want to show their support.

The process of getting adults interested in youth ministry and developing them as volunteers is often full of frustration. When adults hesitate to volunteer or say "no," we often wring our hands, shake our heads and admonish them for not being committed. We cry, "We want adult involvement, not excuses!"

Volunteer Youth Workers: Recruiting and Developing Leaders for Youth Ministry will help ease the sometimes frustrating task of recruiting volunteers. This resource gives suggestions on:

●keeping your youth group highly visible to attract potential volunteers

●involving adults and parents

●developing, caring for and maintaining volunteer youth workers

Volunteer Youth Workers traces a step-by-step process of adult involvement in a vital youth ministries program. This book is punctuated with hands-on tools such as involvement materials, job descriptions, case studies, sample letters, evaluations, and ideas on publicity and high-visibility events.

We will help you understand how Rose Mary became a volunteer youth worker and how you can recruit volunteers in your church. Several lines from Rose Mary's story are highlighted in Chapter 2 followed by helpful hints to use in your youth group.

WILL THIS WORK WITH THE SMALL CHURCH?

The steps and hints for recruiting and developing volunteers are adaptable for any size youth group. Often when we read about programs that seem extensive, we automatically assume that those approaches can't work in a small church. Not true with this book. Every idea we present will work and has worked in the small church. Scale down the models to fit your situation by using the following formula:

●Read this book.

●Decide on priorities for you and your church. List them. For example:

1. involve parents
2. plan for recruitment
3. build a team

●Make a plan. Decide on how much time you are willing to spend on each priority or when you will have accomplished each one.

●Begin the process of recruiting volunteers.

●Evaluate every 30 days with another worker on how well you are following your plan.

●Remember: If you try to do everything, you may end up doing nothing. Pick out one thing and do it well. When you have handed that off to capable volunteers, move on.

All churches, no matter what size, can benefit from this book. As Christians we are one. We are all responsible for each other. We all have gifts though they may be different. We are asked to serve. **Volunteer Youth Workers** is a must for anyone who believes that adults should be involved in youth ministry.

"For just as the body is one and has many members, and all the members of the body, though many, are one body, so it is with Christ. For the body does not consist of one member but of many" (1 Corinthians 12:12, 14).

—J. David Stone

CHAPTER 1
Rose Mary's Story

◆

When my husband, Don, and I were looking for a church to join, we attended services at several churches. One Sunday as we were visiting a particular church, we noticed an excitement in the air—a feeling that "something" was happening. I didn't know right away what that "something" was, but it was there.

As we took our child Toby, who at that time was one year old, into the nursery, we were met by an attractive, smiling young high school girl. She took Toby from my arms and began talking to him. She seemed totally confident in handling him. I felt assured that I was leaving him with someone who really cared. As we left the nursery for the sanctuary, we peeked into some of the other classrooms and noticed there were other young people working with the children—telling stories, talking and playing.

We entered the sanctuary and were welcomed at the door by two young teenage boys nicely dressed in suits and ties. Each had a carnation in his lapel. The boys handed us a bulletin and one of them ushered us to a pew. There was a light chatter going on among the people in the sanctuary, but at the same time there was a feeling of reverence. I immediately felt at home and a part of things.

As the choir entered the sanctuary, everyone stood. *I looked over the congregation. It seemed that the whole front part of the church was filled with members of the youth group. This seemed odd to me as I recalled my high school days in the youth group—we always sat in the back rows and wrote notes.*

At first I thought it was a special Sunday service recognizing the youth group since the members were so involved, but as the service continued there was no mention of a special event. As the pastor read the announcements, however, he told of a mission project that was being led by the youth group members. They were going to help a community build a new church. The pastor also announced several other projects in which the youth group was involved.

Don and I were interested in this energetic church, so we attended a few fellowship activities to learn more. One activity was a "Church Nite" dinner. As we entered the lobby, we were surprised to be met by a group of the young people dressed as clowns. They wore brightly colored costumes, funny wigs and broadly painted smiles on their faces. They were giving directions to those of us who didn't know where to go or the customary way to do things. The clowns then entertained the children as we stood in line to get our meals. *After picking up our plates, we noticed other members of the youth group were dressed alike in blue gingham shirts and navy pants or skirts. They were there to help those who needed assistance—the* children, the elderly and others. They helped us find a place to sit and also served coffee and tea throughout the meal. *Youth were everywhere and involved in everything!*

I will never forget the first Sunday evening worship we attended. Again, as we entered the sanctuary, the youth group was sitting together in the front. The service began with one of the teenage boys from the youth group playing the guitar and singing a beautiful song he had written.

Announcements were given by a youth group member. Next was the "Youth Speak Out," a regular part of the Sunday evening worship. A young girl stood up and told about what the church meant to her and the strength she drew from being a part of the youth group. Following the sermon, the lights were dimmed and candles glowed at the altar table. Someone began playing the guitar and singing softly. It was a special time as one by one the young people stood, walked to the altar and knelt in prayer. As each finished his or her time with God, another would take his or her place at the altar until everyone had an opportunity to kneel in prayer. I remember whispering to Don, "This is where I want my children to grow up."

I then realized the special "something" that made the church different and exciting: It was the young people. The youth group was living, showing and sharing what it truly means to be Christian—to be Christlike. I wanted to be a part of that. I wanted my children to be a part of that, too, and to grow up in a church in which the young people played such a vital role in the total life of the congregation. We joined the church that night.

We soon received an Involvement Card to fill out and return to the church office (see Chapter 4). We completed the information about our family and also indicated that we would be interested in working with the youth group.

Don had his chauffeur's license; he checked on the card that he could drive the church bus. I didn't know what I could do or how I could help the youth group, but I knew I wanted to be with them; I just wrote, "Interested in working with youth."

One evening, not long after we had returned our Involvement Card to the church office, the telephone rang. It was the youth minister from the church calling to make an appointment to see us about our working with the youth group. We readily agreed to meet with him, and we set a time for him to come to our house.

That youth minister was David Stone. When David visited us, he talked about the mission project in which the youth were involved. He said there would be several groups building a church and that there was a need for adult workers to drive the bus and help supervise. David indicated it was not going to be an easy task and asked us to prayerfully consider working on the project. He promised to contact us again in a few days.

After David had left, Don and I discussed how pleasant it was that we had not felt pressured into making a commitment. We prayerfully considered working with the youth, and I made arrangements for someone to take care of Toby. I decided I couldn't wait for David to call us back, so I telephoned and told him we wanted to work on the project.

We began to work and spend time with the group. David became our mentor and helped us become a part of the youth group. It was frightening for me at first to be labeled "youth worker." I didn't feel qualified to serve as a volunteer to a youth group. But the responsibilities we were given were never overwhelming. We met on a monthly basis with David and the other youth workers for prayer and Bible study and to discuss problems that we weren't quite sure how to handle. We divided, shared and rotated responsibilities. We each had specific tasks to do such as serving as "meeter greeters," supper supervisors, game area counselors or care watch volunteers (see Chapter 4). I knew that unless I was there, my task wouldn't get done. I began to realize that I really was needed and that I did have something to give to the youth. I became more self-confident and wondered why I had been so frightened.

As we continued to work with the youth, David recognized our gifts and encouraged us to use them. Don began to coach the church basketball team; he already was coaching in high school. He taught a Water Safety Instructor course to the youth so they could become qualified as life-guards. We taught swimming lessons to the children of the church. I took a calligraphy class that was offered at the church and began to work with the youth media team on making sing-along slides. I began to use aerobics with the youth. These were activities we already were doing in our lives, simple pursuits that David recognized as gifts and helped us develop into something that could be shared with the youth. Our gifts were nurtured and supported until they blossomed far beyond our expectations.

That's my story—it can be your story, too. Join David and me as we draw from our experiences to direct you in recruiting, developing and maintaining volunteer youth workers.

CHAPTER 2
Youth Visibility

◆

Youth were everywhere and involved in everything!

Christianity is caught, not taught. The same is true for recruiting adults to work in youth ministry. The excitement of working with youth is caught, it can't be taught. That is why the visibility of your youth group is so important. In order to discover and develop talented adults, we must have an opportunity to meet them and see them in action with young people. Observing which adults mingle well with youth during high-visibility events will help with volunteer selection.

The volunteers we are looking for should be catalysts for youth to have a relationship with Christ. First, we want adults who love God, Christ and young people. Second, we want adults who maintain good human relation skills and like what teenagers do. If we can find adults with those attributes, then we will have discovered potential leaders. Then, knowing who these adults are and what they do, we have to recruit them.

Recruiting is not always easy. Many misconceptions surround youth ministry: Some adults don't understand youth; they somehow believe that adolescence is a disease and are afraid they will catch it. Since it is a human characteristic to support the things we like, youth ministry must be presented in routine, non-threatening ways. We can do this in a variety of high-visibility settings:

WORSHIP SERVICES

One of the obvious places that high visibility for youth can take place is in the worship services. Simply sitting together as a group can make an impact on the congregation. However, the impact of that visibility must be positive, not negative. For example, perhaps your youth group sits together now in the back row or balcony. That's not unusual, but it doesn't help make youth ministry visible. Whether your youth group is large or small, you will have a definite positive impact on the congregation by having your youth sit in front.

Share with your youth group the vision you have about adult support and instead of trying to remove them from the balcony forever, merely ask, "For the next five Sundays, sit in front with me during the worship service."

The youth group members probably will do so, since it is for such a short interval and because you are doing it with them. If the youth group sits in front for five weeks, it is likely that the action will become a ritual for them. Seeing the young people sit together in front is impressive not only for the regular congregation, but also to visitors. Remember Rose Mary's story:

I looked over the congregation. It seemed that the whole front part of the church was filled with members of the youth group. This seemed odd to me as I recalled my high school days in the youth group—we always sat in the back rows and wrote notes.

Before you know it, there will be a sense of pride welling up in the youth group as the pastor and the congregation privately and publicly affirm the "fine youth group."

There are, of course, many contributions to worship

services that youth can make in addition to just sitting together. Why not get permission for some of the youth to be properly trained to usher and then arrange for them to fulfill that responsibility once a month? Or, each week a different young person can participate in the worship service—sing a solo, read the scripture, lead an affirmation of faith, lead in prayer or give a personal testimony.

Before each weekly worship, the youth group members can pray for the pastor and the worship service. This action not only builds ties with the pastor and congregation, but serves as a model of what Christians ought to be doing.

NURSERY

Youth who volunteer to work in the nursery are highly visible to adults. Enlist various adults (nurses, doctors, parents, child care workers, psychologists, and so on) to train youth to perform the function of Sunday morning child care workers. Not only does this enhance the visibility of youth at the church, but it also provides a valuable service ministry. The training and nursery care can serve as a certification of private, well-trained baby sitters. We make a list of trained baby sitters available to the young parents in our church. This activity builds more community within the congregation and serves as a source of income for teenagers of our group.

FELLOWSHIP DINNERS

There is nothing more delightful than to be served dinner by an energetic, well-groomed young person with a smile on his or her face. A waiter/waitress team of young people wearing similar uniforms (jumpers or smocks) is a refreshing change from going through the line in an impersonal way.

After picking up our plates, we noticed other members of the youth group were dressed alike in blue gingham shirts and navy pants or skirts. They were there to help those who needed assistance . . .

Why not organize a group of youth who would like to learn how to serve meals at various dinner functions of the church? That experience could pay off if you contact area caterers and convention center personnel and tell them of your youth group's availability to serve dinners at public functions. The youth group members would already have the training and might even have uniforms. This is an excellent example of high visibility in both the church and the community.

SPECIAL EVENTS

Annual church picnic. This yearly event is an excellent opportunity to take advantage of the teenagers' love of the outdoors. Youth enjoy being active, running contests and performing. An event which is held annually becomes a ritual that church members eagerly anticipate.

An ideal time for a church picnic is at the end of summer vacation just before school reopens. This helps bring back some of those folks who have gotten away from the routine of Sunday services because of summer vacations and involves the youth in a project which will bring them together for the beginning of a new school year.

Include the youth in the total church planning of the picnic, then let them take responsibility for organizing games for children and performing as clowns.

Galilean service. This inspirational activity can be done at a lake-side retreat, camp or picnic to simulate Jesus preaching from the boat to the crowds on the shores of Galilee. The person fulfilling the role of Jesus is rowed across the lake while the youth group is singing, watching the sunset and worshiping.

When the boat is close to the shore, the speaker gives an inspirational sermon. Afterward, the speaker is rowed away.

Christmas program. The youth take responsibility for

arranging a live nativity scene complete with a stable, animals, manger, Joseph, Mary and Jesus. Wise men or perhaps a choir of angels could make up a live singing Christmas tree. This activity can be presented on the front lawn of the church. Call or send written news releases to all the area newspapers, television and radio stations to invite the community to visit the live nativity scene.

Family retreat. Bring your youth and parents together to plan a retreat in which the whole family attends a camp. This could be for a weekend or just a day. The youth are responsible for games and other outdoor activities such as a "quiet time walk in the woods" as an awareness meditation of God's natural beauty.

Easter sunrise service. The youth plan and present this service for the entire congregation. They then prepare and serve a pancake breakfast before the regular Easter morning church service.

Evening at the church. Invite all new or prospective church members to a candlelight dinner in their honor. The youth serve as hosts and hostesses and top off the gathering with a media/slide presentation of church activities that involve people of all ages. Include choir, activities for youth, meetings, picnics, etc. Help an interested young person prepare a taped narration of the slide show or make a video presentation with background music relating all the activities that are available for new members. An upbeat and positive media presentation can make a favorable impression and will tend to make people want to be involved—sometimes the new members volunteer before you have a chance to ask them.

SUNDAY SCHOOL
AND VACATION CHURCH SCHOOL

Children want to grow up. The constant cry is that Sunday school is boring. The youth group members can help ease the boredom by "adopting" children, making monthly visits to church school classes and being pen pals.

Involving youth group members in the younger kids' Sunday school helps draw the church community closer together, and at the same time provides teaching relief, anticipation and, of course, visibility.

A well-planned vacation church school during the summer months should include youth in many leadership functions—tour leaders, storytellers, song leaders, musicians, recreation leaders, and so forth. Take numerous pictures to post on the church bulletin boards—show the congregation the extent of youth involvement in your church.

YOUTH ANNUAL REPORT TO THE BOARD

When the time comes for reports to be made to your board or education committee, why not let the youth participate?

This is one of the best opportunities that a youth department has to let the church "hierarchy" know that the youth not only exist but have a function and are full members of the church.

If your church does not schedule youth reports to the board, you would do well to help that happen. We suggest you visit with the pastor or the chairperson of the board to make those arrangements.

When you have the go-ahead, spend extra time to make your presentation the best ever. Several young people can use slides, video or posters to aid in the presentation.

We remember in one of our presentations we were reporting on our 50-mile bike hike in which 70 teenagers pedaled from Shreveport to Mansfield. As we told about the hike, our youth in their "bike garb" pushed their 10-speed bicycles through the board meeting room. We only had eight bicycles there, but as each youth would push one bike out the door another youth would take over and push it back into the room. We rotated those bikes during the entire announcement. The board graphically saw youth ministry. It was impressive seeing all those young people and bikes. Everyone left the meeting that night knowing we had an active bike team.

PROJECTS

Sometimes when the church plans projects, it leaves the youth out. As a youth group, do not make that type of mistake and neglect to involve the church committees. If your youth want to participate in a mission trip or project, involve your mission committee from the church in the planning and implementation.

It will bolster the mission committee members' feelings to have made a contribution, and it also will give the youth visibility. Constant reminders from the pulpit, talks to church school classes and receiving the blessing from the board are necessary.

It's difficult to take a group skiing in Colorado and call it a mission. However, all trips serve to bring the group closer to each other because of fellowship, and closer to Christ because of Bible studies. If you are genuine about the trip and the purpose, and have committee approval and support, then the visibility exceeds any negative reflections that might be cast on it. Educate the laity as to the reasoning behind your actions. Communicate!

CHURCH OFFICE STAFF

The church secretary and other staff members will be appreciative if a few volunteers from the youth group help with mailings or take responsibility for painting, cleaning or setting up for meetings. The attitude of the church staff is important. In fact, it's imperative that the staff have an appreciation of the youth group. An ever-so-often, well-placed comment to them about a youth victory or achievement is considerate. Write occasional thank-you notes to staff members or make a "thank you, staff" poster. Encourage the youth group members to stop by the office and give personal thank you's, too. Visibility!

Think about it. The people who attend the functions we just mentioned usually are the active, key adult leaders in the church. If we can help them feel comfortable with youth and let them see the teenagers' natural creative vitality and enthusiasm at work, then they will want to be a part of this special ministry. That's to be expected. Youth group visibility attracts the "movers and shakers" of a congregation. When you have the "movers and shakers" leading your youth group, watch out! Others will want to follow and take part.

George Gallup Jr. and David Poling in their book **The Search for America's Faith** reported that people tend to join a church because of a dynamic youth program. That not only corroborates our experiences, it validates our position.

The excitement of youth ministry should be caught by new members seeing the youth group in action or old members wanting to contribute. Ideally, a pastor or youth leader should not have to push very hard to get quality volunteers. The following story illustrates this point:

There was a pastor in a small Midwestern town whose church may have been typical of many churches we know. The members were slow to make any decisions because they had "always done it this way." They believed the preacher ought to just preach, visit, and conduct funerals and weddings. It must have been a disconcerting experience for that pastor as he tried to motivate the congregation every week.

One day the pastor's secretary noticed that every Thursday the pastor would leave the office about 4 p.m. indicating that he was going home for the day. Several times the secretary had called the pastor's house at 5 p.m. to give him a message only to discover that he hadn't made it home. She became suspicious that something wasn't right since she knew he lived only 10 minutes from the church. With some concern, she persuaded the church board chairman to talk with the pastor about this inconsistency. The board chairman, rather than confront the pastor face to face, decided to follow him one Thursday afternoon. As usual at 4 p.m. the pastor left the church and drove out to the country with the board chairman following at a safe distance to avoid detection. The pastor pulled off the road near a railroad intersection and parked his car. He sat there for some time. Finally a lonely freight train chugged into view, whistled and then rumbled out of sight. After a few moments, the pastor started his car and drove home. The board chairman was puzzled. For several more Thursdays, the board chairman followed the pastor, who each time returned to the railroad crossing. Then one day the board chairman confessed to the pastor that he had been following him and asked him why he would drive to that railroad every Thursday, watch the train pass and then go home. The pastor insightfully, though reluctantly, said, "After working every day in this church, I just need to see something that moves with power that I don't have to push!"

We believe youth ministry ought to be like that powerful freight train. We shouldn't have to push it. It should move because people have become infected with the saving knowledge of Jesus Christ. Youth ministry should be exciting, thrilling and move itself through the highly visible activities described in this chapter.

CHAPTER 3
Leadership Discovery: Handing It Off

◆

Discovering volunteers is quite different from using them. Many youth leaders make the mistake of finding volunteers and then seldom utilizing them. "Doing it yourself" seems to be easier than delegating responsibilities. This chapter shows you how to gradually delegate responsibilities with a minimum of effort until volunteers are in charge. This process of gradually handing over responsibilities is called the Four Phases of Leadership. Following the description of the Four Phases are two case studies, and ideas for further training and equipping of youth workers.

THE FOUR PHASES OF LEADERSHIP

Is there anything more frustrating than attending a youth meeting and not knowing who is in charge? We believe that the basis of any leadership discovery, recruitment or training that has any long-lasting validity must revolve around one designated, self-appointed or elected leader. The genesis of leadership discovery is at the point of one person being in charge.

Phase One: I do it. Regardless of what you have heard in seminaries, workshops or other educational circles, we are confident that before delegating authority or responsibilities, the person in charge should "go first." That is, do it yourself. We're sure you're familiar with the saying, "If you want it done right, do it yourself." There is a truth to that statement. How can people know what you want them to do if you do not show them? We believe that this principle applies to all of youth ministry. The following story is an example of how David began the process of handing over leadership with Phase One:

> As a youth director, I knew I should be conducting a Bible study. I had advertised for someone to step forward and lead, but no one would. At least the ones I felt comfortable with theologically wouldn't. So, reflecting on that familiar saying, I thought, "I will do it myself!"
>
> Phase One got under way as I determined the date, time and place for a weekly Bible study. *I* made the announcements, *I* put up notices on the bulletin board, and *I* made the punch and cookies for after the Bible study. Not only that, I called the youth to remind them of the new study and prepared the Bible study lesson *myself*.

Phase Two: You and I do it. When someone sees you involved in an activity and relates to it, you have a potential leader. We look for leadership possibilities any time we have an activity going on. When we see someone in the activity who shows an unusual interest or ability, we not only make a mental note of it, we affirm that person by making mention of it in some way.

As time goes on and it becomes apparent that person loves God and has a definite skill in youth ministry, we usually invite him or her to share the leadership. Most of the time the person will agree to do so for two important reasons: The person is asked to do something that he or she knows how to do, and the person is asked to do it with someone else.

Back to David's story:

> When everyone had arrived at my house on that first Tuesday evening, I began the meeting by thanking the young people and adult volunteers for coming. I felt the evening studies would flourish and that the group would grow in faith and closeness with one another. I asked that the participants turn in their Bibles to 1 Corinthians 12:12-27 to begin a study on the body of Christ. I noticed amid some chatter, confusion and questions concerning, "Are there extra Bibles?" and "Is that in the Old or New Testament?" that Barbara, an adult volunteer, had already turned to the passage. Her Bible looked as if it had been through two world wars and barely survived. As I looked closer, I could see that many of the verses in that passage were highlighted in several colors. I also noted comments written in the margins. I got the distinct impression that she had studied this before. I was surprised, though, when I saw her study Bible since it was from a different, more fundamental approach than mine. But I thought, "We can learn from each other."
>
> Following the Bible study that night, I asked Barbara to stay for a few extra minutes. She

agreed and I asked her to help teach the Bible study the next week. I was delighted when she agreed to do so. We met later that week to study together and plan for the next Bible study. A rich relationship developed as Barbara and I studied and planned together. Instead of an apparent confrontation over whose theology was correct, we proceeded in an atmosphere of love that brought us to the third phase of the Four Phases of Leadership:

Phase Three: You do it, I will support. One of the major mistakes we make in handing off leadership is to dump responsibilities onto someone's lap. We are so glad to get rid of the work that we do not take the time that is necessary to educate, explain or even say, "Thank you, I will be praying for you." It is more like we "prey" on others rather than "pray" for them.

After working together with our new recruit, we can usually determine when it is time for us to step aside and allow him or her to take control of the leadership. That is what this third step is about—the gradual handing off of the responsibility. When the time comes to let the person fly on his or her own, ask the volunteer to take charge and say that you will be close and supportive. That is important. Stay close. Support.

Back to David's story:

> Barbara and I developed a close relationship through that Bible study. Not only did we become close friends, but our faith and openness to God's leading developed at an enormous pace. I knew Barbara would not do anything that would be harmful to anyone in the Bible study. She now

had a model of human relation skills and an appreciation for another point of view. I challenged Barbara to take over the responsibility for leading the Bible study and assured her that I would be available for any assistance she might need. We still had the study at my house, I made the cookies and punch; I was there, but Barbara planned and presented the Bible study.

As the weeks passed, I found myself engrossed in several other important facets of youth ministry. Realizing that Barbara was capable of flying by herself and not worrying about what and how she was leading the study (after all, I had been there and had shared with her for several months), I asked Barbara to move into Phase Four.

Phase Four: You do it, I will move on. Phase Four may be the hardest phase to move into, possibly because of ego. It is difficult to let a baby go after you have birthed, nursed and raised it. It's human nature to want to maintain control all the time. It is also selfish. If we seriously want to hand off leadership, then Phase Four is a must. Part of the genius of the Four Phases of Leadership is that you discover people who can do a better job than you do. Instead of letting that be a threat, make it a victory. More people will be involved in the youth program because of its many opportunities for involvement. Conceptually, all will be in concert because you handed it off in an organized, gradual process. Not only will the word "burnout" disappear from your vocabulary, but "excitement" will take its place.

Back to David's story:

Barbara finally said "yes" to taking over the Bible

study. Although I do not participate in that Bible study anymore, I do hear how it is going when Barbara reports at the monthly team meetings. (We'll tell you about team meetings in Chapter 6.)

CASE STUDIES

The following two case studies are examples of how David discovered, recruited and handed off the leadership to volunteers. See if you can get the feel and direction to proceed with your own program in developing the Four Phases of Leadership.

Papa John: Right here, right now. John D. had been a member of our church for a year when I met him. He regularly attended church with his family; in fact, John sang in the choir and two of his children were in the youth group.

I had just moved to the church and was eager to get something moving in the youth department. I had an acute interest in a performing youth music group that would be different from the traditional choir. I wanted the choir to perform all types of music and be a touring group to sing for secular organizations as well as for churches and church-related activities. There did not seem to be any kind of model to follow, so I just began with Phase One: I do it.

I wrote letters with rehearsal information and sent out announcements in the church publications that a performing youth music group was being started. Soon rehearsals became a weekly event and the young people were not only singing well together, they were having great fun.

The months went by and the "Cheerful Givers" were born. At first they traveled in cars to nearby churches and performed for any group regardless of size or time. As the group became more sophisticated, we added a sound system. Soon we knew we needed a lighting system.

About this time, John came into the picture. John's daughter Michele was in that first group and John would come to pick her up after rehearsal each week. It was not long before he peeked in to see what we were doing. One day as we were discussing the lighting possibilities and our need for a spotlight, John said, "I'll help you make a spotlight from an automobile headlamp." Presto! Not only did we get our spotlight, but an operator, too.

We soon discovered that John was an engineer. The business of handing off the ministry became more like taking over as John became the technical adviser to the Cheerful Givers. Because of the mass of equipment that we had put together, Bill (a student) was attracted to help out with the lights and sound.

Staying true to the concept of the Four Phases of Leadership, John handed the responsibility off to Bill. During the time, John and company had taken over almost everything else concerning the Cheerful Givers. So I felt John was ready to be the overall coordinator for them and I could move on to other needs.

I must admit, saying goodbye was not easy. I had started the group, worked with it through five albums, several national tours and a national television show. People were really noticing the group. Reluctantly, I turned the leadership of the Cheerful Givers over to John and in so doing stayed true to the system.

Not only did the Cheerful Givers flourish without me, its next tour was to England. And I stayed home. John became "Papa John" to all the Cheerful Givers. I must tell you that when I got over the ego hurt, my heart swelled bigger than ever before and I felt a quiet sense of satisfaction knowing I had been doing God's work and not my own.

There are "Papa Johns" in every youth group. Look for them. We must be aware and sensitive to the fact that potential volunteers are "right here, right now," if we want to hand off the ministry.

Russ: Diamond in the rough. I became exasperated

with one parent who called me after every event to complain that his child did not enjoy the program, the project or the trip. My initial reaction was to say, "Okay, keep her at home then!"

Fortunately, I talked with a friend about Russ' constant complaints. My friend suggested that perhaps Russ was volunteering to work. I voiced my concern: "That's ridiculous! Anyone who would complain so much surely isn't interested in working. He's just interested in making trouble." When my friend asked why Russ would be trying to make trouble, I began to think: "Maybe I am dealing with the symptoms instead of the problems. Perhaps what Russ is saying is that he can do things better."

I began to investigate Russ. I asked people who knew Russ about his strengths and learned that most impressions of him were extremely good, not bad. Russ was a churchman. He was an active member of an ecology group called the Sierra Club. He was quite a family and often took his entire family camping.

I asked Russ for an appointment to talk about youth ministry. He readily agreed. He probably thought he would have a chance to pin me down on an issue. Instead, I beat him to the punch. I said, "Russ, how about helping run the camp-out next month in the Kisatchie Forest?"

He looked puzzled, then asked, "What do you want me to do?" He was hooked. He took over the backpacking, eventually the canoeing, and finally became our outdoor recreation youth worker. I never heard another complaint from him. I had discovered a diamond in the rough.

FURTHER EQUIPPING
AND TRAINING OF WORKERS

The Four Phases of Leadership are a tremendous process for the development of workers. However, those of us who are leaders need to continually be on the lookout for additional resources to equip our volunteers. We can do this in several ways:

Watch for specialized workshops. Denominational district, conference and diocesan training events are often free and usually have good leadership and programs. Check with your denominational office for information and invite all interested volunteers to attend.

Join with youth group volunteers from other churches for programs. If you do not already attend a youth workers' fellowship or ministerial alliance, find out about these offerings in your area. Usually the programs are not doctrinal, but strictly educational-process oriented. If there is not such a fellowship in your area, consider this an invitation and motivation to get one started.

Invite experienced leaders to team meetings. As you meet other leaders, read about them or hear reports from those you respect, invite those leaders to special meetings with your volunteers. It is important to broaden the perspective of your volunteers by giving additional exposure to other ideas, thoughts and concepts.

One of the most damaging things that can happen to a youth group is when a leader burns out. Burnout occurs when one repeatedly does something with no new input. To avoid burnout, we must provide opportunities for our leaders to be "on the furrow, not in the ruts." That is why it is important to provide for additional resources and training opportunities for our volunteers.

CHAPTER 4
Building a Team

♦

Armed with an understanding of the Four Phases of Leadership and examples of how to recognize the gifts and skills of the congregation, we are ready to begin building a team of volunteers. Let's remember that a team is a group of people pulling together for a common goal. In order that we have a winning team, we must find people who love God, love youth and like what youth do. We must discover these people, recruit them, let them know what is expected, and provide care and maintenance. Above all, remember to use volunteers and their skills once you have recruited them. If a team is to function, we must let them get into the game.

DISCOVERY

The best way to discover volunteers in the typical church is to look for those who are doing the job now. Youth ministry must be the most important job there is. You must be sold on it or you will discover quickly that no one wants to be on a losing team with an unenthusiastic coach. Look for winners. Winners are people who are making it happen within God's grace and glory. Look for those who are taking charge of the spaghetti suppers and setting a record of attendance. Ask *them* to be volunteer youth workers.

Be on the lookout for adults who really seem to get along with the youth and whom the youth like. Watch them interact on several occasions. Ask questions about the adults. Check out their credentials. All the preliminary work you do will enable you to build a team that has a solid base.

As you observe adults interacting with your young people, begin to make a list of those you think are good prospects. Make notes on your list such as "Mr. Jones really listened to Jamie when she was telling him about the upcoming program." It will not be long until those notes will be merely mental because you will have developed the practice of recognizing the characteristics that are exceptional for working with youth.

Another way to discover volunteers is by the Involvement Card. When people join your church, be sure they have an opportunity to immediately fill out a card. Take a snapshot of the new members for the church newsletter as a way of introducing them to the congregation.

Involvement Card

Name _____

Address_____

City_____State_____ZIP_____

Phone (Business)_____(Home)_____

Age (Please circle one):

18-25   26-35   36-45   46-55   56-older

Rank the following (1 is the activity you most enjoy; 7 is the activity you least enjoy):

[   ] leading groups   [   ] hosting meetings
     (teaching, organizing)   [   ] furnishing transportation
[   ] providing support needs   [   ] driving the church bus
[   ] record-keeping   [   ] visiting and telephoning

Special skills you have:

(Bus driver, musician, mechanic, cook, computers, finances, children, youth, young adults, adults, etc.)

1. _____ 2. _____
3. _____ 4. _____

[ ] I would like someone to call on me *right away* concerning how I can become involved in the church.

Work experience in the church:

Please list some previous churches, tasks and dates of involvement.

_____
_____
_____

Also discover potential youth workers by having adults in your congregation fill out the following Adult Involvement sheet once a year. You'll be surprised at the interests and talents some people have and are willing to share.

Adult Involvement

Teach:
____ Sunday school
____ Sailing
____ Canoeing
____ Repelling
____ Swimming
____ Cardiopulmonary
    resuscitation (CPR)
____ Lifesaving
____ Guitar
____ Dance
____ Karate
____ Tennis
____ Bowling
____ Ground school for pilots
____ Calligraphy
____ Special craft _____
____ Special skill _____
____ Special sport_____

Lead:
____ Exercise/aerobics
____ Singing
____ Recreation
____ Bible study
____ Share group
____ Hiking
____ Telephone committee
____ Other _____

Coach:
____ Basketball
____ Flag football
____ Softball
____ Volleyball
____ Other _____

Loan my:
____ Darkroom
____ Boat (type) _____
____ Home (for after program
get-togethers)
____ Camp/lake house
____ Pickup truck
  ____ with driver
  ____ without driver
____ Computer
____ Video cassette recorder
____ Video or other camera
____ Slide projector
____ Film projector
____ Motor home
____ Swimming pool for
parties
____ Ice cream freezer
____ Copy machine
____ Light table
____ Graphic arts supplies

Assist these teams:
____ Bicycle
____ Drama
____ Child care
____ Host/hostess
____ Choir or music
____ Paper staff
____ Ushers
____ Video/media
____ Creative movement
____ Outdoor
____ Clown
____ Puppet
____ Substitute (fill in where
needed in emergency)

Other:
____ Prepare snack supper
____ Prepare refreshments for parties
____ Help prepare meals for retreats
____ Make homemade ice cream
____ Provide decorations for special occasions
____ Drive for carpool
____ Conduct survey
____ Help with workcamp project
____ Photography
____ Play instrument _____
____ Work with social concerns project
____ Plan/design treasure hunt
____ Public relations: write articles for local newspaper, make
posters, radio or television announcements
____ Help with fund raising
____ Serve on parent/teen relationship panel
____ Work on retreat

_____ Operate _____ video cassette recorder
                   _____ film projector
                   _____ slide projector
_____ Use my influence with public officials, government, school
_____ Provide fish for fish fry
_____ Supervise light construction
_____ Provide child care for youth workers
_____ Assist in program planning
_____ Youth sponsor
_____ Bus committee _____ driver
                     _____ maintenance
_____ Involvement counselor
_____ Youth newsletter
_____ Answer telephone _____ hours from _____
                       _____ day(s) week M T W TH F
                                        (circle one)
_____ Telephone committee
_____ Volunteer _____ typist
                _____ receptionist
_____ Provide scholarships for youth who cannot afford money for retreat/trip
      $25 $50 $75 $100 $_____ (circle one)
_____ Serve as lifeguard for swim parties
_____ Serve as chaperon for parties
_____ Adopt a youth for discipleship
_____ Help with school study night (once a week)

Use the forms for involvement. When tabulating volunteer information, the first order of business is to appoint an involvement counselor. This person is responsible for setting up a committee to collate all involvement forms and make a list of the names of those that were not turned in. He or she also is responsible for organizing all volunteer workers and making sure that the volunteers are notified as to the date their services are needed. Not to use a volunteer will be defeating your purpose of getting people involved. Remember, no gift is too small that it can't be used.

The next step is to examine the existing program and special events. Make a list of all the needs: human resources, materials and locations. Put the needs on a calendar. Review the Adult Involvement list and make assignments. (A computer makes volunteer assignments easier.)

The involvement counselor should send out notices of assignments to the volunteers. The involvement counselor also should let the chairperson responsible for any event know who will be helping out or providing for a need—the chairperson can contact the volunteer with further information if necessary.

RECRUITMENT

Whenever you have a prospective volunteer for a task, go ahead and ask. If the task is something he or she has previously volunteered to do on an Involvement Card or questionnaire, be sure to give a definite term or length of commitment. For example, if you are recruiting someone to lead a 12-week Bible study, tell him or her it is for 12 weeks only. If you want the volunteer to teach for a year, let him or her know. If you are recruiting a youth worker for one event, be sure you spell that out or you may be stuck! (It works both ways.) At any rate, when you recruit someone, assure the person that it is not a lifelong commitment.

Sometimes people volunteer for things they do not know how to do, but think they would like. You can help make them successful. Monitor them early and affirm their progress and product. If they need help, you will be there; if not, your encouragement will keep them interested. Just remember the guidelines from the Four Phases of Leadership—stay close and support.

When recruiting people for teaching jobs, adviser positions or any other long-term responsibility, go see them in person. Here are a few basic rules to follow:

1. Make an appointment. Any job worth doing

deserves your personal "eyeball-to-eyeball" approach. Once you have made your "pitch," it is difficult for the person to tell you "no" face to face.

2. Prepare carefully.   Do not go into a meeting un-prepared. In advance, prepare copies of the materials, a time schedule, and a commitment to a plan, as well as build enthusiasm about his or her participation. This could make a difference in a "yes" or "no" answer. By being prepared, you are telling the potential volunteer that he or she is important to you.

3. Overcome the objections.   There are just so many objections about any one thing. Think ahead about what the objections may be and be prepared to answer them. For example:

> Objection: "I don't know where I'd find the time."
>
> Response: "I realize you are a busy person and there are just so many hours to a day, but I be-lieve youth ministry is important enough to ask you to rearrange your priorities. Let's talk about the time I'm asking for and the time you have available—maybe we can work something out."
>
> Objection: "I don't know anything about it."
>
> Response: "I didn't either my first time out. You won't be doing this alone. We have regularly scheduled volunteer meetings and a wealth of re-source materials. We also have training sessions and workshops for your assigned task. With your love of God and commitment to youth, I have no doubt that you will soon be feeling comfortable in your role. The fact is that people are more impor-tant than programs. Was it a person or program that introduced you to Christ?"

Before recruiting volunteers, have in your own mind the answers to any objections the prospect might voice.

If possible, it is best to test prospective leaders in a situation before inviting them to do any long-term work with the youth group. For example, Don and Rose Mary served as volunteers for a mission trip with 20 youth before David asked them for a long-term teaching commitment.

The following dialogue is a reconstructed transcript of the recruitment interview with Don and Rose Mary. David thanks them for their help, asks them to volunteer for teaching positions, overcomes an objection and waits for their response.

> David: I just wanted to tell the both of you thank you again for the wonderful leadership that you gave our senior high on the mission trip. You really won a lot of friends and touched many lives. It is neat to see a young couple such as you who care so much about youth that you will give your vacation time to work with them.
>
> Rose Mary: It was fun. I felt like I received more from them than I gave to them.
>
> Don: We learned a lot about the young people and grew really close to them.
>
> Rose Mary: We had some great kids in that group. We had the best ones.
>
> David: I've discovered that when you have time to really get to know kids that the natural tendency is to fall in love with them. That's what happened to you and that's what happened to them, they fell in love with you.
>
> That's part of the reason I came to see you. I want to tell you how much I appreciate you and how much the youth responded to your leadership. The other reason is I would like for the two

of you to consider teaching, on a weekly basis, our ninth grade Sunday school class. It would require a strong commitment for you to teach it like you would want to see it taught. I have some suggestions that would make it not only easier as far as your preparation time is concerned, but would be a tremendous Christian growing experience for you.

Don: What do you mean?

David: We provide weekly opportunities either at noon on Tuesday or 5:30 p.m. Thursday for our teachers to get together to talk about the upcoming lesson. You or Rose Mary could come to that meeting.

Rose Mary: David, I don't feel that I'm qualified to teach a Sunday school class. We just joined the church and I know nothing about the background of this denomination. Besides that, as far as attending the teacher's meetings, I don't know that I could find someone to keep the baby.

David: That's what is so exciting about you and Don teaching together. You don't know it all, but your enthusiasm, your love for those kids and your wanting to learn more about God in your life make for a great combination. I believe it is the relationship that we build with the young people that is more important than the program. Let me ask you this, was it a person or was it a program that influenced you to Christianity? My hunch is that it was a person. Am I right?

(Don and Rose Mary both nodded their heads.)

And you've already started building those relationships.

As far as the baby sitting is concerned, I've made arrangements for the church nursery to be open during the time of the teacher's meeting and Sunday school classes.

The time commitment for teaching is one year—from the first Sunday in September through the last Sunday in June. I know I'm asking for an incredible commitment, but that's what it takes to really affect the lives of kids. We will furnish the resources and opportunities for training and your own personal growth, and I want you to come join our Christian education faculty.

Because it is an incredible commitment, I would like for you *not* to give me an answer now. Look over these materials I brought to you and prayerfully consider this request. I am going to come back to see you next Tuesday. If you have any questions between now and Tuesday, don't hesitate to call.

Rose Mary: David, we're going to have to give this a lot of thought before we can say yes.

David: I know. Thanks.

Do not, under any circumstances, back down from the fact that it takes an incredible commitment to work in the church youth ministry program. Tell the prospective volunteers you want nothing but the best. That's why you're there. Be specific about the time frame in which you want them to work. Assure them that it will not be for life. Many volunteers have said "yes" but not had a specific time frame for the length of their service. There are some bitter, lonely people stuck teaching and counseling that do not know how to get out. Those volunteers are also ineffective.

4. Do not ask for an answer now. So often we feel that we have to receive an answer immediately because the need is so pressing. Wait. The preparation to recruit someone is important and takes time. If properly done, your visit

with the potential youth worker will be a matter of presenting a challenge to him or her and probably one that requires
prayer. In closing the presentation, say something similar to
the closing conversation between David, Rose Mary and
Don.

5. Follow up. Contact the potential volunteer when
you said you would. Some people will be so excited, like
Rose Mary, they will call back before you have a chance to
do so. Most will wait to answer until you call them. If potential volunteers say "no," be sure to thank them for their
consideration; if they say "yes," proceed with the next step.

6. Give specific assignments. Remind the volunteer of the job description and time commitment. One of
the most frustrating aspects of working with youth is to volunteer for a job but not be told what is expected or how to
proceed.

The following Sunday Evening Program Agenda is for a
youth group of 25 to 50 members. Included in the agenda
are descriptions of the program activities. Following the
agenda are job descriptions for the youth workers for this
type of program. Whether you are planning to recruit a
classroom teacher or an evening program volunteer, each
one needs a job description for his or her own clarification.
Use these descriptions to aid you in writing job descriptions
for your specific needs.

Sunday Evening Program Agenda

5:00 p.m.   **Sign-in:** Registration, games and contests—all junior
and senior high age levels.

5:30 p.m.   **Ring-up:** This is a ritual in which everyone (including the janitor and cook) participates by putting
arms around each other and making a gigantic circle.
During ring-up we usually sing an appropriate song
such as "Let Us Break Bread Together" or "They'll
Know We Are Christians By Our Love." We pray and

then have a big "crunch" as everyone takes two steps forward and squeezes the person next to him or her. Everyone pays $1.50 for the theme supper which follows the ring-up.

6:00 p.m. **Happening:** All young people and youth workers get together following supper for a sing-along and series of skits, stunts and regular features such as the following:

● *Pastor-on-the-spot:* The pastor sits on a chair and responds to a question regarding the previous week's sermon. This is done in good taste. It also involves the pastor or one of the associate pastors on a regular basis in the youth group and highlights his or her sermon. An alternate idea is to ask the pastor's views on a certain subject. Whatever you do, make it dramatic like a television show so as not to put anyone on the defensive (have someone announce the pastor and field a question similar to a zany, enthusiastic television announcer).

● *Huggy Bear time:* This is a fun time in which a person dressed as a big teddy bear enters during the middle of the program and shouts, "Do you know what time it is?"

Everyone answers, "It's Huggy Bear time." The bear reminds everyone that we need at least eight hugs a day for maintenance and 12 hugs to grow; the bear then leads the group in getting caught up on their hugging quota. During this hug time, a John Philip Sousa march or other upbeat music is played.

● *Speak-up school:* In this brief activity an athlete, cheerleader, student council representative, principal, teacher or student says a positive word for God and suggests a way in which the young people can be more Christlike in school. The speaker can be videotaped if he or she is unable to be there in person.

● *Speak-out Christian:* Representatives of the junior and senior highs stand before the group for a couple of minutes and tell what the youth group has meant to them.

● *The closing:* Everyone is included for a ring-up

and announcements. This is also a time for a prayer and another group "crunch."

●A regular visitor to the Happening is the "Party-Goer" who makes announcements about the social functions and opportunities for the week. She always dresses extravagantly and drawls out the announcements or introduces another person who makes additional announcements concerning the socials. "Professor Ourloveovereverything" is another regular visitor to the Happening; he points out a particular youth or adult who has shown God's love in the past week. By the end of the year, he notices a good attribute of everyone in the youth group.

6:30 pm.	**Meeting time:** Junior highs to Room 201, senior highs to Room 101.
7:15 p.m.	Ring-up in each area.
7:30 p.m.	Reach out/worship in sanctuary.
8:30 p.m.	Altar prayer time/dismissal.

Youth Worker Job Descriptions
For the Sunday Evening Program

Sign-in: Set up the registration table by 4:45 p.m. and remain until relieved by the late care watch volunteer.

Supervise registration by having each member complete a blue card and each visitor complete a yellow card. Following registration, give all visitor cards to the youth minister. Post the other cards on an attendance chart in the office.

Early care watch: Responsible for patrol and security from 4:45 to 6:30 p.m.

Late care watch: Relieve sign-in volunteer and stay until everyone is in worship or has gone home.

Other care watch responsibilities include the areas inside and outside the activities building.

●Unless given permission, no youth should leave the building after having checked in until the time for the evening worship.

●All outside doors shall be locked at all times.

●Keep youth in assigned areas only.

Game area: Responsible for opening game areas. Have games and equipment ready to be checked out from the team office on the first floor. Return all equipment at the ring-up time.

Mingle with youth and help involve them in various games. Look for the loner and challenge all who come into your area to play. Don't allow horseplay or disrespect of game area. Close all areas by 5:30 p.m.

Equipment/announcements: Stationed in the team office to make announcements. Play music over the P.A. and assist with equipment checkout.

Sound/lighting: Set up the P.A. with four microphones in Room 101 by 5:30 p.m. Set up a spotlight in the back of the room with an operator.

Mingler: Mix with all youth—especially notice new youth or loners.

Theme supper: Plan a theme dinner for Sunday program. Find help for cooking, setting up and cleaning up.

Coordinator: Assimilate all volunteer assignments and make sure everyone remembers his or her job. Send the assignments to each volunteer two weeks before the program.

—Extras—

●All counselors will get their own substitutes from a list furnished by the youth department if they have to miss an assignment.

●Following are suggestions for theme suppers: Mexican buffet, Hawaiian luau, "steak-on-a-stick" (country), "foo yong Sue," ranch steaks and barbecue, Texas chili cookoff, "Louisiana-style crawfish boil," Boston tea party (baked beans and tea), "little Italy" (pizza or spaghetti), dinner at Japan's "Benny ha-ha's," "food and a friend" (bring a buddy).

Following is a youth worker sign-up sheet for the Sunday evening programs. Circulate the sheet at the once-a-month volunteer meetings (see Chapter 6). It is completed verbally and each person is asked to take a turn at the particular assignments with which he or she feels most comfortable. The positions are rotated each meeting.

After the volunteers have agreed to do jobs, the volunteer coordinator for the program organizes this list and sends it to each youth worker about two weeks before his or her assignment.

Sign-up Sheet for the Month of _____

Position	Name	Phone Number
Sign-in		
Early care watch		
Late care watch		
Game area (need three)	1.	
	2.	
	3.	
Equipment/announcements		
Sound/lighting		
Mingler (need two)	1.	
	2.	
Theme supper		
Coordinator		

Following any event at which an adult provided a service or his or her possessions, someone (preferably a youth who was involved in the event) should be responsible to write a personal thank-you note. Not only is it a common courtesy, it also will build allegiance to your program.

Whenever we use someone else's belongings such as a motor home, we should constantly remind the youth and adults to treat it as a sacred trust. The motor home should be cleaner when we return from the trip than before we left. The tank should be filled with gas. Leave a letter, scroll, or banner inside with notes of appreciation from those who used the motor home. Never take volunteers for granted—treat them with appreciation and respect.

DISMISSING A VOLUNTEER

Dismissing a volunteer is not easy; however, occasionally you may make a mistake and recruit the wrong person for a job. What do you do? In the first place, remember the volunteer is a child of God—dismissing him or her should be the last resort. Pray for guidance in the issue and thoroughly think through the situation. Did you clearly communicate the job description? Have you given the volunteer enough guidance and direction? Have *you* faced up to *your* role in the failure?

Discuss the situation with an impartial observer such as the senior pastor. If you conclude that you should dismiss the volunteer from the current position, decide whether the person would work well in another task with the youth program. If not, is there another church-related activity for the volunteer?

Assuming that you have explored every possible way to salvage this worker and the bottom line is "he or she has to go," then these are our recommendations:

Make an appointment with the worker at his or her home or office, or on common ground such as a restaurant. Over lunch or coffee affirm the worker as a person and then say that you feel he or she would be better suited in another job. Be honest. Do not waver. Care enough to tell the youth worker that it is not working out and tell him or her why. We have found that most people who are not doing a good job know it and seem relieved when we tell them.

Do not ask the worker to stay on until you find a replacement. You must be ready to replace him or her or live without the position filled until you recruit someone else.

When you have dismissed the worker, be sure you follow up with affirming kinds of contact. For example, write a thank-you note for his or her service or visit with the person for coffee or lunch.

To continue to have a warm relationship with that person is important to you and for him or her. Remember, do not dismiss someone unless it is the last resort.

CHAPTER 5
Involving Parents

◆

A team of volunteer youth workers is not complete unless parents are given an opportunity to be included. The parents of your young people fit into several categories: parents and youth who are active church members, active parents with inactive youth, or inactive parents with active youth.

We believe that if a youth comes to church, his or her parents (no matter which category they fall into) should be actively involved in some way. There are *no* exceptions. If you make any, then you diffuse whatever positive accomplishments that already have been done for the youth program.

Remember "Papa John" in the case study in Chapter 3? He was an active church member with a daughter who was already active in the youth group. We remember involving John even further when the church finally decided to buy a bus. The youth group had been collecting Green Stamps for months and had enough to pay for half the purchase price.

The bus was an old Trailways model with more than one million miles, but it had been refurbished. The purchase price was $12,500, and we had to pick it up in Atlanta. Finding someone who could drive a big bus like that was not easy. That was when Michele's dad, John, spoke up, "I can drive anything that has wheels, and I worked on big diesels in the Navy." After arranging schedules and transportation to Atlanta (750 miles away), I recruited John to make the trip to get the bus.

Everyone at the church was excited. We were getting a Trailways bus. John arrived in Atlanta, got a two-day briefing about the care and maintenance of a big bus, and set out on his trip home. ("Papa John" would eventually become known as "Big John" because he sat on that "big" seat and drove that "big" bus.) By the time John got home, it seemed that the ownership of the bus had changed. You would have thought that he was the new owner. He would hardly let anyone else touch it, much less drive it.

John readily accepted the chairmanship of the bus committee. It was not long before driver's qualification tests and rules were set up, and a careful maintenance schedule was organized. "Big John" had found another niche. As you can see, parents are recruited in the same manner as other adult volunteers. We recognized a gift and called it forth—the enabling process.

DISADVANTAGES TO INVOLVING PARENTS?

Although the story of John is a positive one, sometimes there are disadvantages to involving parents. Many parents are content to be followers and are only too glad to help or not help. There are some parents, however, who claim to know everything and want to plan, implement, and dictate what the youth should and should not do. If you are not a strong leader, you may get run over by a well-meaning parent who has a strong personality or influence with others in the church. When we notice that personality type, we flinch, then realize that we are not the targets. We begin to spend as much time as we possibly can with that parent to build a friendship so that the parent knows where we are coming from.

If you have a parents' organization, make sure *you* stay in charge of it and that the bylaws do not encompass program planning for you. Keep the parents' participation as support teammates, not dictators.

Occasionally, parents will volunteer who you might deem as "undesirable." Work hard to find tasks for them to do—even the seemingly most undesirable person has a contribution to make. The task probably is not where they would ideally see themselves, but if you find a place for them, it will usually fill their desire to be needed and of assistance.

Sometimes, if we have not done a good job of preparing young people for parental involvement, the youth may say that they do not want their moms or dads involved. We honor that and do not ask the parents. However, we are aware that the real reason for hesitation is that the youth do not know how their parents will be accepted by their peers. So we gradually work the parents in by asking them to do little things within a meeting such as "John, would you get the lights?" or "Susan, could you hand me the chalk?" By showing acceptance on our part, the idea that the parents can make a contribution begins to be more acceptable to the young people.

Many youth will tell you they do not want parents at their meetings. Likewise, many adults will hesitate to volunteer and tell you they do not think youth want them at their meetings. If every youth's parent is expected to be at one meeting a year, not only will it be natural for parents to be involved, but young people will actually be excited when their parents or other parents attend. When parents are excited about a program or the way it is being run, their youth are too. If a youth is complaining about something, you can bet the parent is too. It works both ways.

THE PROGRAM

Many of the disadvantages to involving parents can be overcome with the proper attitude and preparation. Overall, any program that has 100 percent parent involvement will be dynamic, positive and productive. It is our business to come up with ways to involve the parents and not readily excuse their lack of involvement. It is a must to understand this if this program is to work. We understand that you may not get 100 percent involvement, but that has to be your goal. Why go for less?

An objective of youth leaders everywhere should be to get the parents of youth group members actively involved in some way and have them come at least once a year to a youth program as observers. The following steps will help you involve all parents.

1. Make a list. Gather the names of active and inactive youth and their friends. List the names of each youth with the names and addresses of his or her parents. You may even want to code the list to denote such things as divorced parents, living with mom, and so forth. Make a chart such as the following illustration and post it in a prominent place in your office or where you will be able to easily see it.

Youth Information Chart

Youth	Parents	Phone	Visit Date	Response	Involvement

LEGEND

A Active in youth group	* Active youth member's parents
I Inactive in youth group	● Divorced, living w/mom or dad
C Constituent (friend)	+ Inactive church members

The chart can be built as a permanent structure with cup hooks in each block to hold round tags. This will enable you to keep the chart updated and neat.

2. Send a letter. The message in the letter to parents should convey that in your church all parents are expected to be involved in the youth program in some way. Also, advise them that this is their opportunity to sign up on the Adult Involvement sheet (see Chapter 4) for one or more ways that they can be involved. Ask them to indicate on the Parent Observation form which date they would like to visit a youth group meeting.

Letter to Parents

August 10

Dear Parent,

This time each year, we in the youth department send out two forms for parents to complete. The first is an Adult Involvement sheet for you to use to select several ways that you want to be involved in our youth ministries program this year.

The second form is a list of Sundays during the school year. This form also must be returned so that we will know which Sunday you will be visiting our youth group. We require that you visit at least one time a year.

Because we use these forms to plan our total program for the year, we must have them returned no later than _____.

I look forward to hearing from you soon.

Yours in ministry,

J. David Stone
Youth Director

Parent Observation

Please mark your choices for visiting our youth group. Rank first, second and third choices. We will coordinate all parents' requests and let you know your observation date for one of our Sunday programs. (You'll notice we give ourselves a few weeks off during the summer.)

SEPTEMBER	OCTOBER	NOVEMBER	DECEMBER
___ 9	___ 7	___ 4	___ 2
___ 16	___ 14	___ 11	___ 9
___ 23	___ 21	___ 18	___ 16
	___ 28	___ 25	___ 23
			___ 30
JANUARY	**FEBRUARY**	**MARCH**	**APRIL**
___ 6	___ 3	___ 3	___ 7
___ 13	___ 10	___ 10	___ 14
___ 20	___ 17	___ 17	___ 21
___ 27	___ 24	___ 24	___ 28
		___ 31	
MAY	**JUNE**	**JULY**	**AUGUST**
___ 5	___ 2	___ 7	(off)
___ 12	___ 9	___ 14	
___ 19	___ 16		
___ 26	___ 23		
	___ 30		

Note: You will need to change the dates to meet your schedule.

3. Publicize what you are doing. The more aware the church is of what you're doing, the more support you will receive from outside the youth department. Arrange for the pastor to make a series of weekly announcements from the pulpit.

There is *power* in the pulpit. Do not forget that. An announcement from the pulpit will do wonders that all your calling may not even begin to match. The following is a series of announcements that we suggest be used from the pulpit.

This first announcement should be made the Sunday before the parents' letter goes out:

It's that time of the year again when we need to begin planning for our next year's youth program. In order that it be the best ever, (name of youth director) is mailing out forms this week to all parents of youth. Please complete these forms as soon as possible and return them to the church.

The second announcement should be made the Sunday following the mailing of the letter:

Some of the Adult Involvement and Parent Observation forms have already been returned, thank you. If you have not completed your forms, please do so as soon as possible and get them in. If for some reason you haven't received your letter and forms, please let someone in the youth office know right away.

The third announcement should be given the week before forms are due:

All Adult Involvement and Parent Observation forms *must* be turned in by next Sunday. Assignments and programs are being planned for the year and every parent is expected to have a part. If you have misplaced your forms or have not received them, please contact the church office right away.

Announcements should be made weekly in the church newsletter and bulletin as well as in any youth publication. The text of the announcements should be positive, always stressing the importance of parent involvement and the necessity of planning head. You may paraphrase the announcements made from the pulpit. Just stay positive.

Posters made by youth along with testimonial letters by parents posted on the bulletin board will help get results. Make sure that the letters are first-class—not just thrown together at the last minute. Young people have terrific creative abilities. Let them help out and watch for a potential leader—perhaps someone to be in charge of publicity for the youth.

Another fun way to publicize the youth group is by presenting a video or live skit to Sunday school classes, dinners, board meetings, prayer groups or to the congregation during a worship service.

Do not overlook the power that youth have over their parents. Selling this program to your youth group can have fantastic results not only to get parents involved, but to build a community attitude with youth that their parents are wanted, needed and important. Do not just say to youth, "Remember to tell your parents to complete the forms." Have a program which highlights contributions that parents have made the past year such as loaning their cabin site for a retreat, furnishing transportation or food, making homemade ice cream, providing scholarships for unfortunate kids who could not otherwise afford the retreat or camp, etc.

Youth participation in skits and planning for a special program can be a major key to parent response to your letter and involvement. Parents need to know that their youth want them involved.

4. Day of reckoning. This is the most important day in the entire program—the day that psychologically makes the plan work. This is the due date for all forms to be turned in to the office.

Even with the announcements and publicity—all of the forms are not going to be in. Reasons for this include: low interest; parents think you are not serious; parents forget about the forms and leave them on top of the refrigerator in the "to-do" pile; or parents think "someone else will do it, my small involvement is not that important."

You must meet those objections head on. During the week before the deadline date, organize a task force of parents and youth to help follow up on the day of reckoning. Figure that you will need one person for every four who do not turn in their forms. For large congregations, the task force might have to include many people. Ask your task force members to meet with you for 30 minutes following the Sunday worship and give them their assignments in a short training session.

Provide them with a packet which includes:

●A list of names and phone numbers of the parents they are to call.

●Four copies of each of the two forms that were sent.

●A sample message they are to make over the telephone. For example:

> Hello, Mr./Mrs. _____. This is _____ from the youth task force. The Parent Involvement and Observation forms are due in the church office today because our planning begins tomorrow. In looking over the forms that have come in, I noticed yours was not here. I assume that it may have been lost in the mail or got misplaced in some way. At any rate, I would like to bring another form by for you to complete this afternoon or evening. It will only take a few minutes. When would it be convenient for me to come over? Now, later this afternoon or early evening?

A Sunday afternoon or evening would be the best time to call and get the forms completed. If it is not possible for your task force to go by and pick up the forms, complete the forms over the phone. Stress that your task force is to be upbeat and positive—not overbearing.

Request that your task force return all forms to you by noon the following Monday. You will be surprised how well this approach works and with a minimum of hostility, too. The next year the parents will be more educated as to the importance of the involvement forms and a much larger percentage will turn them in before the day of reckoning.

5. Follow up.   After the day of reckoning, immediately send letters to all parents thanking them for their response and assuring them that as the program is worked out for the year, they will receive their assignments. It is important to acknowledge that you know they want to be involved and that you are going to use them.

Follow-up Letter

Dear _____,

   We have received your Adult Involvement and Parent Observation forms. Thank you for being willing to serve as _____ or provide _____ for our youth department. Assignments are in the process of being made now for your observation day. Your involvement assignments may take longer. However, as soon as we have completed our scheduling, we will be contacting you. Again, thank you for your love of youth.

In Him,

J. David Stone
Rose Mary Miller
Youth Directors

This letter should be handwritten. If the number to be written is too numerous, then use a computer to personalize it as much as possible. Using a computer can also save time and involve others. Ask a volunteer to loan his or her computer to write the program.

With or without a computer, the involvement counselor and a team of other adults collate the material. All parents who have volunteered their services or possessions are contacted with a telephone call and/or a letter. The time and location are specified along with what the volunteer is to do. For example:

Dear Mr. Mason,

As you recall, on the Adult Involvement sheet, you offered to furnish your motor home for a youth event. Our youth are planning a trip to the Smokies to help with an Indian mission. We will be driving all night going out and coming back. Could we please reserve the motor home for March 18 to 25. Pastor Brent is going with us and will be in charge of the motor home. He will contact you next week. Thank you for your participation in our youth program.

In Him,

Gary Hamilton
Parent Involvement Counselor

6. The calendar. The involvement counselor then combines all information from the Adult Involvement sheet with the names and dates from the Parent Observation form onto a calendar. (The involvement counselor should try not to schedule more than three sets of parents to observe at any one program. More than that seems overwhelming.)

A copy of the calendar is mailed to each volunteer parent with his or her volunteer service, possession or observation date highlighted. Thus it becomes a visual-psychological tool to help motivate attendance.

Highlight of a Calendar Segment

17	18	19
PARENT OBSERVATION *Meet at the main entrance of the youth building at 6 p.m. Mr. and Mrs. Campbell Mr. and Mrs. Jones Mr. and Mrs. Norman	YOUTH MISSION TRIP *Meet at the church at 4:30 p.m. Mr. Mason—motor home Mr. Hopkins—tools	

A spinoff of the calendar procedure is a contagious attitude of involvement on the part of the parents. They see the names and involvement of other parents and want to become involved themselves.

The following step continues from this point to show how to involve the parents in the Sunday evening program in which they act as observers.

7. Observation day. The week before the parents are scheduled to visit, put an announcement in the church newsletter or bulletin naming the parents who will be visiting. That little reminder is also a small pressure point to help assure their participation.

Create a host/hostess committee of youth to write notes stating their pleasure that those parents will be visiting. Include in the note a time and place to meet for the Sunday program. Sometimes a call to the parents is adequate, but the formal note is a more effective reminder of the date and location.

Note for Observation Times

Dear Mr. and Mrs. Campbell,
   We are looking forward to your visit at our youth group this Sunday night. We are busy making special tags for you and making plans to host you.

Mary Ward and I will meet you at the main entrance of the youth building at 1611 Brevard St. at 6 p.m. After we have a snack supper together, we will watch "The Happening" and then on to the senior high program, "Do Grandmas and Grandpas Really Count?" Following the program at 7:30 p.m. we will attend our evening worship service. Dr. Moore will preach on "Being the Kingdom of God."

We are looking forward to having you visit with us. See you at 6 p.m. Sunday.

In Him,

David Kilgore
Chairman of Host/Hostess Committee

Arrange observations so that at some point during the year, every youth in the group serves as host or hostess. Acting as a host or hostess builds relationships between adults and youth, and it also gives youth a valuable boost to their self-confidence.

When the parents arrive to observe, the host or hostess should greet them and hand them a handcrafted name tag. Sometimes the name tags are weird, but never dehumanizing. They might be in the form of a typical homecoming chrysanthemum made from crepe paper with long streamers and a note written on the inside: "Don's Mum."

The parents are escorted to the ring-up circle; they hear the usual comical announcements about the upcoming week and we say grace. Following the ring-up, the parents are escorted to a table where the host and hostess serve them supper and then visit with them.

Following supper, the parents join the Happening. The host or hostess stays with the parents for the rest of the evening. It is at this time the parents are introduced to the youth group. This is done with high energy fanfare and is carefully calculated to excite everyone without embarrassing anyone. After the Happening, parents are taken to the respective program (senior high parents to the senior high program, junior high parents to the junior high program).

A special area is set aside to seat the parents. We stress that they are to be observers only; they always comply. The parents join us for the final ring-up, goodbyes, and closing prayer which includes thanking God for parents. The parents are squeezed and hugged with the rest of the group.

Remember: Visibility is the key to attract volunteers and gain support—the same is true for recruiting parental support. Parents should have an opportunity to see the activities their teenagers are involved in: games, songs, Bible studies, fellowship, sharing, etc. When youth ministry is presented in an enjoyable, highly visible, non-threatening way (such as an observation day), parents and adults are most likely to give their 100 percent support.

CHAPTER 6
Care and Maintenance Of Your Team

◆

Your youth ministry team of parents and adults is one of the most important items of any youth ministries program. Properly cared for and maintained, it will give you more support than you could ever want; poorly cared for and maintained, it will be your downfall.

AFFIRMATION IDEAS
You have said your team is important, now act like it. Youth are not the only ones who need affirmation and a friend in time of need. The adults you are working with do, too. Look for opportunities to tell them you noticed something they did well such as the way a worker handled a youth trying to sneak out of a program. Seize the opportunity to praise the youth worker and ask him or her to teach the other adults how to handle such discipline situations.

Publish a weekly newsletter of youth group activities and information. Choose a "Youth Worker of the Week" and in the newsletter print a noteworthy effort he or she makes or has made. Ask the pastor or board chairperson to write the youth worker a letter of appreciation.

Avoid public put-downs for counselors as well as youth. Take private time with your volunteer youth workers to offer suggestions or help in dealing with situations you think they may have handled poorly.

Once a year conduct a "Volunteer Appreciation Week" in which *all* volunteers are recognized at a Sunday morning worship service. Send personal invitations to each volunteer for a special recognition of his or her service to the church. At the service each volunteer can stand or be called forward and presented with a certificate of appreciation or perhaps a "Very Important Person" pin.

Recognize an adult who has made a special contribution and on cue all the youth can give him or her a standing "O"vation. All youth stand with their arms over their heads in the shape of an "O" and say, "OOOOOOOOOO!"

Hold an annual, thematic "Sunday School Teacher Appreciation Dinner." One year we had a "Cinderella Ball" theme dinner. As the guests arrived, they were greeted at the door by one of the youth dressed in a rented tuxedo. They then were escorted one at a time to the entrance of the dining area. There the guests were greeted by another young person who introduced them, "Ladies and gentlemen, may I present our seventh grade Sunday school teacher, Mary Williams!" Then a trumpet was sounded, "da-da-da-daaaaaaa!"

We *must* realize that our job would not be successful if it were not for the people who give their time and gifts to be there when we need them. It is imperative that we let them know how much they are appreciated.

VOLUNTEER YOUTH WORKER MEETINGS

It is difficult to get people together. Once a month is not too often, however, if you are working to have a meaningful ministry. We think it is good to set aside one evening a month to have all the youth workers to a home for dessert and to discuss their questions, concerns and joys of working with youth ministry. Rotate the home meetings sites for this monthly visit. Try to keep the meetings short.

It is important to begin each meeting with a focus on Jesus Christ. Each month a different counselor can give a brief devotional. Allow for a discussion of the youth program, and be sure to give positive verbal reinforcement to everyone for a job well done.

Take time to talk about the sign-up sheet and get everyone signed up (see Chapter 4). If your youth worker team is small, double up on the responsibilities or eventually try to double the number of team members.

Your volunteer meeting will keep the air clear and let you know of any emerging problems. Failure to conduct regular meetings gives the volunteers the impression that there is not a forum for their concerns and frustrations, so they begin talking among themselves.

Here is a suggested format for monthly meetings for youth workers:

Volunteer Meeting Format

7:00 p.m.	Arrival at the meeting site home.
7:15 p.m.	Greeting and appreciation to host and hostess.
7:20 p.m.	Short devotional by one of the volunteers.
7:30 p.m.	"State of the Union Address." Youth director tells of upcoming plans, squelches rumors, affirms workers and gives thanks.
7:45 p.m.	Open discussion, questions and thoughts.
8:00 p.m.	Volunteer assignments for upcoming month.

8:10 p.m.   Prayer adjournment.
(Usually a ring-up time and prayer of going forth in commitment.)

8:15 p.m.   Dessert and farewell.
(With a large group, several people can be responsible for bringing desserts.) A homemade ice cream social is always a winner in the summer. This monthly meeting has a potential of becoming a gourmet's dessert delight.

THE VOLUNTEER RETREAT

Once a year, your youth workers deserve an all-expense-paid retreat. It is not a time of planning for the new year. It is not just a fun time. It is a retreat—an opportunity to regroup, get to know one another better, and get the feel of what youth ministry at your church is really all about.

Mix in the following ingredients for your youth worker retreat:

1. Personal spiritual evaluation. Everyone needs a chance to reflect. Personal morning devotional, vespers, benedicting silence, planned quiet walk down a wooded path, or a structured time of journal-keeping can be of immense value.

2. Overview of the youth program. The use of slides; videos; movies; testimonies of counselors and teachers; letters from youth, parents, and even members of the community will help to tell the story of youth ministry in your church. All who work with youth need to see the big picture and how they fit in with their particular gift. This overview should be fast-paced, underlined with moving music and brought to a climax with a beautiful story or challenge such as what the youth group did for one person or the impact the group can have on the entire community.

3. Information, education and inspiration. Fifty miles away there is another youth director, minister or speaker who can challenge your workers with new information about youth, give a new concept of education and who can inspire them to greater heights. Such a speaker should be scheduled to speak each day during the retreat—his or her stimulating input is needed.

4. Introduction of one another and your total church staff. Playing together may be the best way to get to know each other. Plan games and events in which no one loses and everybody wins. One of the best ways to develop relationships and appreciation is to invite the church staff to share in at least part of the retreat. From the custodians to the ministers, it is important that your workers see the visible appreciation from the church staff for them and the youth program. Treat the whole event as a family get-together.

END OF THE TERM

We take for granted the work of our volunteers. Our tendency is to say thank you to those who do a superior job and give a sigh of relief when those who do a so-so job are through. We need to focus on the concept that all those who volunteer do so because of a heartfelt need and perhaps a tug from God. Although a thank you may not be necessary for them to hear, it is something we feel we must do to complete the whole transaction.

Letter of Appreciation

Dear Alison,

We would again like to say thank you for the valuable service you have rendered our church as _____.

We continue to hear people compliment your ministry.

Because we value you and the gifts you have to share and because we want to provide the best possible environment, training, and resources possible for others, we would like for you to complete the enclosed evaluation and return it in the self-addressed, stamped envelope.

Again, thank you for all you do and for who you are in the Lord.
In Him, we really are One,

Wayne Moore
Youth Minister

All volunteers should have an opportunity to evaluate the program at the end of their terms. By "putting ourselves on trial" with feedback from their evaluation forms, we gain new insights and affirmation, and we avoid getting stagnant.

An evaluation from someone who has just completed a term seems to be a proper as well as a revealing way of making new discoveries and keeping ourselves honest.

Evaluation Form

Name _____

Address _____

City_____State_____ZIP _____

Position served _____

Length of term _____

On a scale of 1 to 10, rate the following statements with 1 being the lowest score, 10 the highest.

1. I found the task that I did to be the same as what I was recruited to do.
   1 2 3 4 5 6 7 8 9 10
   Comment _____
   _____

2. During the term of my work, I received the promised support from other leadership.
   1 2 3 4 5 6 7 8 9 10
   Comment _____
   _____

3. Training and learning opportunities were available to me during my term.
   1 2 3 4 5 6 7 8 9 10
   Comment _____

   _____

4. I was informed about the resources that were available. They were adequate for me to complete my task.
   1 2 3 4 5 6 7 8 9 10
   Comment ._____

   _____

5. I was personally cared for and nurtured through this term by my leader.
   1 2 3 4 5 6 7 8 9 10
   Comment _____

   _____

6. I would be available in the future to:
   a. Serve in the same capacity again.
   b. Help train other leaders.
   c. Work in another area of ministry such as _____
   d. Help recruit other workers.
   e. Other _____

7. Additional comments:

Thank you for your candid and honest evaluation.

EPILOGUE

◆

Discovering, recruiting, and training adults and parents for youth ministry is a ministry in itself. We need each other to be effective volunteer youth workers—besides, there is more fun and security when we are doing youth ministry together!

We urge you to back off from your workaday world and examine the whole picture. Look at the possible resources available to you in the people in your church and in your life. Call on them. Give them the benefit of the doubt. Ask God for guidance and build a team of volunteer youth workers.

We are promised that ". . . in everything God works for good with those who love Him, who are called according to his purpose. We are more than conquerors through Him who loved us" (Romans 8:28, 37).

Claim this promise. Your ministry will be blessed and your heart filled, because you are not alone.

—J. David Stone
—Rose Mary Miller

ACKNOWLEDGMENTS

◆

Many people are responsible for the advent of **Volunteer Youth Workers: Recruiting and Developing Leaders for Youth Ministry.** We wish to express appreciation to those hundreds of people who have prodded us until we gathered this material in written form and for all the volunteers who have been through this process. A thank you to Group Books for its confidence and sense of urgency. Thank you to the editor of Group Books, Lee Sparks, for his counsel and assignment of Cindy Hansen to our book. Special thanks to Cindy Hansen, our editor, for her personal concern that this important work be correct and complete, and for her constant updating and affirmation. And finally, our appreciation goes to Bill Ball, our student associate for his support and encouragement in making this book a reality.

OTHER YOUTH MINISTRY RESOURCES FROM

DENNIS BENSON'S CREATIVE BIBLE STUDIES, BY DENNIS C. BENSON. This huge resource offers 401 complete, creative Bible studies for ALL of Matthew, Mark, Luke, John and Acts. 660 pages. $19.95.

COUNSELING TEENAGERS, BY DR. G. KEITH OLSON. The authoritative, complete, and practical reference for understanding and helping today's adolescents. Hardbound, 528 pages. $19.95.

THE YOUTH WORKER'S PERSONAL MANAGEMENT HANDBOOK. Provides unique help for youth workers as they seek to better control and manage their professional and personal lives. Hardbound. $16.95.

THE BASIC ENCYCLOPEDIA FOR YOUTH MINISTRY, BY DENNIS BENSON & BILL WOLFE. Answers, ideas, encouragement, and inspiration for 230 youth ministry questions and problems. A handy reference. Hardbound. $15.95.

THE GROUP RETREAT BOOK, BY ARLO REICHTER. This is the resource for start-to-finish retreat planning, execution and evaluation . . . plus 34 ready-to-use retreat outlines. 400 pages. $15.95.

HARD TIMES CATALOG FOR YOUTH MINISTRY, BY MARILYN & DENNIS BENSON. Hundreds of low-cost and no-cost ideas for programs, projects, meetings and activities. $14.95.

THE YOUTH GROUP HOW-TO BOOK. Detailed instructions and models for 66 practical projects and programs to help you build a better group. $14.95.

SPIRITUAL GROWTH IN YOUTH MINISTRY, BY J. DAVID STONE. Offers help for youth workers to grow in their relationship with God. Also offers incredible opportunities for spiritual growth in youth groups. Hardbound. $12.95.

CREATIVE WORSHIP IN YOUTH MINISTRY, BY DENNIS C. BENSON. An ideas-packed resource for youth worship in various settings—Youth Sundays, youth group meetings, retreats and camps, many more. $11.95.

THE YOUTH GROUP MEETING GUIDE, BY RICHARD W. BIMLER. This resource provides years of inspiration, ideas and programs for the most common youth group activity—the meeting. $11.95.

BUILDING COMMUNITY IN YOUTH GROUPS, BY DENNY RYDBERG. Offers practical guidance and workable ideas to develop a caring Christian youth group. Over 100 creative activities. $11.95.

CLOWN MINISTRY, BY FLOYD SHAFFER & PENNE SEWALL. Everything you need to know to begin a clown ministry or enhance your present ministry. Includes 30 detailed skits and more than 50 short clowning ideas. $7.95.

VOLUNTEER YOUTH WORKERS, BY J. DAVID STONE & ROSE MARY MILLER. A step-by-step process for involving adults in a vital youth ministries program. $6.95.

STARTING A YOUTH MINISTRY, BY LARRY KEEFAUVER. An insightful book with tips on starting a youth ministry program or revitalizing an existing program. $5.95.

THE BEST OF TRY THIS ONE (Volume 1). A fun collection of games, crowdbreakers and programs from GROUP Magazine's "Try This One" section. $5.95.

MORE . . . TRY THIS ONE (Volume 2). A bonanza of youth group ideas— crowdbreakers, stunts, games, discussions and fund raisers. $5.95.

TRY THIS ONE . . . TOO (Volume 3). Scores of creative youth ministry ideas. $5.95.

TRY THIS ONE . . . STRIKES AGAIN (Volume 4). The newest in this popular series. A gold mine of original, simple and fun youth group activities. $5.95.

FRIEND TO FRIEND, BY J. DAVID STONE & LARRY KEEFAUVER. Provides a simple yet powerful method for helping a friend sort through thoughts, feelings and behaviors of life problems. $4.95.

PEW PEEVES. A humorous look at all those little things that drive you crazy in church. $3.95.

Available at Christian bookstores or directly from the publisher: Group Books, Box 481, Loveland, CO 80539. Enclose $2 for postage and handling with each order from the publisher.

109728